D0478698

Upper Plains

Montana
North Dakota
South Dakota

Jim Westcott

Mason Crest
450 Parkway Drive, Suite D
Broomall, PA 19008
www.masoncrest.com

©2016 by Mason Crest, an imprint of National Highlights, Inc.

Printed and bound in the United States of America.

CPSIA Compliance Information: Batch #LES2015.
For further information, contact Mason Crest at 1-866-MCP-Book.

First printing
1 3 5 7 9 8 6 4 2

Library of Congress Cataloging-in-Publication Data

Westcott, Jim.
  Upper plains : Montana, North Dakota, South Dakota / Jim Westcott.
    pages cm. — (Let's explore the states)
  Includes bibliographical references and index.
  ISBN 978-1-4222-3336-8
  ISBN 978-1-4222-8621-0
  1. Middle West—Juvenile literature. 2. North Dakota—Juvenile literature.
  3. South Dakota—Juvenile literature. 4. Montana—Juvenile literature. I. Title.
  F351.W47 2015
  978—dc23
                              2014050201

Let's Explore the States series ISBN: 978-1-4222-3319-1

Publisher's Note: Websites listed in this book were active at the time of publication. The publisher is not responsible for websites that have changed their address or discontinued operation since the date of publication. The publisher reviews and updates the websites each time the book is reprinted.

About the Author: Jim Westcott writes educational content for children. He lives in West Irondequoit, New York with his wife Sue and his two sons, Jack and Andrew. Jim has a masters degree in Special Education from Nazareth College, and worked as a special education teacher outside of Rochester, New York, for 15 years before becoming a full-time writer. The first book in his children's chapter book series *Jack's Tales* was published by Splashing Cow Books in 2015.

Picture Credits: Everett Historical: 20 (bottom); Library of Congress: 16, 19, 31, 34, 53; Montana Historical Society: 14; National Park Service: 32, 52; Brenda Riskey/UND: 44; used under license from Shutterstock, Inc.: 3, 6, 7, 9, 10, 11, 12, 18, 21, 22, 23, 26, 27, 29, 30, 33, 37, 40, 41, 42, 43, 46, 47, 49, 50, 54, 60; American Spirit / Shutterstock: 1; Joyce Boffert / Shutterstock.com: 58 (bottom); S. Bukley / Shutterstock.com: 20 (top), 38 (top), 58 (top); DFree / Shutterstock.com: 38 (bottom); Nagel Photography / Shutterstock.com: 39, 55; Tom Reichner / Shutterstock.com: 36; U.S. Air Force photo: 57; U.S. Geological Survey: 35.

Table of Contents

KEY ICONS TO LOOK FOR:

Words to Understand: These words with their easy-to-understand definitions will increase the reader's understanding of the text, while building vocabulary skills.

Sidebars: This boxed material within the main text allows readers to build knowledge, gain insights, explore possibilities, and broaden their perspectives by weaving together additional information to provide realistic and holistic perspectives.

Research Projects: Readers are pointed toward areas of further inquiry connected to each chapter. Suggestions are provided for projects that encourage deeper research and analysis.

Text-Dependent Questions: These questions send the reader back to the text for more careful attention to the evidence presented there.

Series Glossary of Key Terms: This back-of-the book glossary contains terminology used throughout this series. Words found here increase the reader's ability to read and comprehend higher-level books and articles in this field.

LET'S EXPLORE THE STATES

Atlantic: North Carolina, Virginia, West Virginia

Central Mississippi River Basin: Arkansas, Iowa, Missouri

East South-Central States: Kentucky, Tennessee

Eastern Great Lakes: Indiana, Michigan, Ohio

Gulf States: Alabama, Louisiana, Mississippi

Lower Atlantic: Florida, Georgia, South Carolina

Lower Plains: Kansas, Nebraska

Mid-Atlantic: Delaware, District of Columbia, Maryland

Non-Continental: Alaska, Hawaii

Northern New England: Maine, New Hampshire, Vermont

Northeast: New Jersey, New York, Pennsylvania

Northwest: Idaho, Oregon, Washington

Rocky Mountain: Colorado, Utah, Wyoming

Southern New England: Connecticut, Massachusetts, Rhode Island

Southwest: New Mexico, Oklahoma, Texas

U.S. Territories and Possessions

Upper Plains: Montana, North Dakota, South Dakota

West: Arizona, California, Nevada

Western Great Lakes: Illinois, Minnesota, Wisconsin

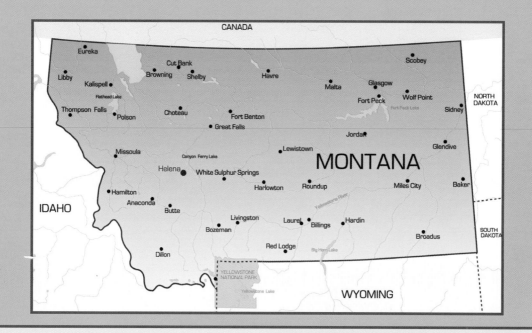

Montana at a Glance

Area: 147,040 sq mi (380,831 sq km)[1].
Fourth-largest state
Land: 145,545 sq mi (376,962 sq km)
Water: 1,494 sq mi (3,869 sq km)
Highest elevation: Granite Peak,
12,799 feet (3,901 m)
Lowest elevation: Kootenai River,
1,820 feet (555 m)

Statehood: November 8, 1889
(41st state)

Capital: Helena

Population: 1,023,579 (44th)[2]

State nickname: Big Sky Country
State bird: western meadowlark
State flower: bitterroot

[1] *U.S. Census Bureau*
[2] *U.S. Census Bureau, 2014 estimate*

Montana

Montana is the "Big Sky" country. This state is not only big, it alo includes some of the best-preserved land and waterways in the United States.

Geography

Nearly 150,000 square miles (380,000 square kilometers) fit into Montana's borders. Only Texas, California, and Alaska are larger in area. However, relatively few people live in this vast state. The population density of Montana averages 7 people per square mile (2.7 people per square kilometer.) Only two U.S. states have a lower population density: Alaska and Wyoming.

To the north, Montana shares a border with the Canadian provinces of British Columbia, Alberta, and Saskatchewan. To the east, Montana borders the states of North and South Dakota. Wyoming lies to the south, while Idaho borders the state in the southwest and west.

Montana's terrain was formed by the activity of glaciers, as well as by the eroding forces of wind and water over millions of years. The state can be divided into two main areas: a flatter region and a higher, drier, rockier region. Montana has many mountains and valleys.

Low, grassy valleys cover large parts of Montana. These valley lowlands stretch for hundreds of miles and offer a spectacular view of snow-capped mountains that push against the low lands and seemingly exist as far as the horizon travels.

The eastern broad valley region contains more prairie and flat grasslands than mountains. The western region is much higher in elevation and combines forests and mountains.

The northwestern part of Montana contains pristine lakes and national parks. Glacier National Park is located in the northwestern part of the state. Throughout the northwestern region of Montana are areas of vast wilderness, towering mountain peaks, forests, and some broad meadows.

Some people consider the scenery of Glacier National Park to be the most beautiful in the country. The plains have an abundance of colorful flowers. The park contains 762 lakes and dozens of waterfalls. Wildlife is abundant: there are 60 species of

 # Words to Understand in This Chapter

basin—a hollow depression or print in the Earth that is lower than the surrounding land.

constitution—a written system of principles or ideas that are used as the basis of government for a state or nation.

hydroelectric—electricity that is generated by water falling or moving through equipment at a dam or waterfall.

reservation—in the United States, a land that is designated as official Native American territory.

skirmish—a brief conflict or fight that does not involve many soldiers.

mammals, including elk, grizzly bears, bighorn sheep, and wolves, and 260 species of birds. Most rivers and streams in Glacier National Park teem with rainbow trout, cutthroat trout, and brown trout.

The Rocky Mountains dominate the landscape in western Montana. The broader mountain ranges in the state include the Flathead, Gallatin, Ruby, Swan, Absaroka, Beartooth, and Bitterroot mountains. A few of these ranges have peaks higher than 12,000 feet (3,650 m).

Bighorn sheep, grizzly bears, and the Rocky Mountain goat live in west-

View of a lake in Glacier National Park, Montana.

The Rocky Mountains dominate the landscape of Montana.

A herd of bison moves along the Firehole River in Yellowstone National Park, as geysers steam in the distance. The bison were nearly hunted to extinction during the 19th century.

A colorful sunrise highlights the fall foliage along the West Boulder River Valley in south-central Montana.

ern Montana. Herds of pronghorn live off of the lush vegetation on the eastern plains. Bison herds once stretched for miles across Montana's plains; today, these creatures live in protected areas like the National Bison Range in Flathead Valley.

Yellowstone National Park was the world's first national park. Yellowstone extends beyond Montana's borders into Wyoming and Idaho. It covers 3,468 square miles (8,983 sq km). Yellowstone is famous for its volcanic activity and hot geysers. Much of the park itself covers a caldera, or low-level volcano that is capable of extremely powerful eruptions (usually millions of years apart). Visitors come to Yellowstone to observe the many natural features classified as volcanic activity, such as steam vents, mud pots, hot springs, and the geysers. The most famous of these is Old Faithful, a geyser that erupts about every 91 minutes, spraying boiling water and steam 145 feet (44 m) into the sky.

Some of the state's larger lakes are located in southeastern Montana. Lake McDonald, Flathead Lake, and Red Rock Lakes are located in this part of the state. Also running through southeastern Montana is the Missouri

A crowd of tourists watches Old Faithful erupt in Yellowstone National Park. The geyser can shoot between 3,700 and 8,400 gallons of boiling water more than 145 feet (44 m) into the air. Eruptions typically last between two and five minutes. Another Yellowstone geyser, called Steamboat, is known for even larger eruptions, but these do not occur as regularly as Old Faithful's eruptions.

River, Montana's largest river. The Bighorn River runs through a Crow Native American **reservation**. The Little Bighorn River is one of Montana's best trout fishing rivers. The White Sulphur Springs are in southeastern Montana. These natural, hot springs consist of pure mineral water. Vacationers come to White Sulphur Springs to bathe in these hot mineral baths. Known for its white water rafting, Smith River, is down valley from White Sulphur Springs.

Vacationers go on dino-hunts in northeastern Montana. The state is rich with the fossils of dinosaur and other prehistoric animals that lived millions of years ago.

Montana receives a low amount of annual precipitation, at 13 inches (33 cm). Summers are shorter than winters, and have average temperatures between about 75° and 85° Fahrenheit (24° and 29° Celsius). The plains of Montana go through cycles of drought followed by periods of heavy rain, which causes flooding. The regions with higher elevation have frost and freezing nearly two-thirds of the year. Here daytime temperatures hover at around 10°F (–12°C) during the winter.

History

Tens of thousands of years ago, Paleo-Indians arrived in North America by crossing a land bridge that once connected Asia (Russia) to Alaska. They traveled along a route known as the Great Northern Trail, which extended from Alaska into the continental United States.

When the Paleo-Indians reached the area of modern-day Montana, they found mountains covered with thick forests, miles of grassy prairies, herds of bison and other types of large animal for hunting, and rivers and streams for trout fishing.

Paleo-Indians were the forerunners of the Native American tribes that would live in the region when the first Europeans arrived. The Shoshone tribe settled in Montana's Great *Basin* region during the 1600s. Next came the Crow, then the Blackfeet, Atsina, and the Assiniboine. These Native Americans migrated to the West from the Great Lakes and Mississippi River Regions.

The Sioux, along with the Cheyenne and the Chippewa, arrived in Montana during the 1800s. The Blackfeet, Assiniboine, the Crow, Cheyenne, and the Atsina lived on the flat, grassy and rolling lands of Eastern Montana. Other tribes, such as the Kalispel Indians, Kietanai, the Bannack, Shoshone, and the Salish Indians, lived in Montana's mountainous areas.

During the 17th century, European countries claimed Montana and other parts of North America. Eventually a few hardy explorers and French fur trappers began to explore the region. During the late 1730s and early 1740s, brothers Francois and Louis Joseph de La Vérendrye entered Montana from Canada, searching for valuable beaver fur.

Spain took control over Montana from France in 1762, but returned control of the vast, unexplored territory to France in 1801. Two years later, the French government sold this

North American territory to the United States. The Louisiana Purchase in 1803 doubled the land area owned by the United States.

Thomas Jefferson, the third president of the United States, was eager to find out more about the vast Louisiana Territory. He sent an expedition commanded by Meriwether Lewis and William Clark to explore the new land, produce maps of the terrain, and catalog its wonders. The expedition started in 1804 and ended in 1806. Lewis and Clark encountered many Native American tribes, and found unusual animals and plants. They explored waterways and marveled at the natural resources.

Lewis and Clark passed through Montana during their exploration of the Louisiana Purchase. The Shoshone woman Sacagawea points the way to the expedition leaders near the Three Forks of the Missouri in this painting by Edgar S. Paxton, which is on display in the Montana State Capitol. The painting also shows Sacagawea's husband Charbonneau (right), and Clark's African-American slave, York.

During the journey, Lewis and Clark engaged a French fur trader and his wife, a young Shoshone woman named Sacagawea (or Sacajawea), to help guide them and speak with the natives they encountered. Sacagawea played a vital role in the success of their mission. She helped the expedition find and prepare food in the wild and successfully guided them to the Pacific Ocean. Lewis and Clark crossed what is now Montana in 1805.

Trappers learned about Lewis and Clark's animal discoveries. In 1807, Canadian explorers John Colter and David Thompson mapped most of modern-day Montana. The areas they explored included much of what is now Yellowstone National Park.

In 1846, a trading post, Fort Benton, was established in Montana. It was located on the Missouri River, so that steamboats could bring trappers and their supplies to the region. The fort was originally managed by the the American Fur Company, but later was sold to the U.S. military.

During the 1860s, John White struck a large gold deposit at Grasshopper Creek. Virginia City, a gold-mining town, emerged from the soil after an even larger gold strike there in 1863. News of miners getting rich brought 10,000 gold miners to Montana towns like Virginia City.

The Sioux chief Crazy Horse led a small army of Sioux and Cheyenne warriors against American troops in June of 1876 along Rosebud Creek. In late June, Lieutenant Colonel George A. Custer of the U.S. Army's Seventh Cavalry attacked an Indian village along the Little Bighorn River. Little did Custer know that he was badly outnumbered by the Sioux and Cheyenne, who attacked his soldiers. The Battle of the Little Bighorn, also known as "Custer's Last Stand," was a major defeat for the American Army. However, the U.S. military was too strong for the Native Americans, and by 1877 the Sioux, Cheyenne, and Arapaho had been forced to stop fighting, give up control of their lands, and move to reservations.

Big Hole Valley in southwestern Montana was the site of another clash between the U.S. Army and the the

This magazine illustration from 1877 shows Chief Joseph of the Nez Perce surrendering to General Nelson A. Miles of the U.S. Army. The Nez Perce were trying to leave the United States and settle in Canada, but were stopped by U.S. forces in the Bear Paw Mountains of Montana.

Nez Perce in August 1877. The Nez Perce, a tribe from Oregon, were trying to escape from the U.S. military because they did not want to be forced onto a reservation. They traveled hundreds of miles, trying to reach Canada. The U.S. Army caught up with them in Montana. Around 40 soldiers and 80 native warriors were killed at the Battle of Big Hole. The Nez Perce were stopped short of their goal, and eventually had to move to a reservation in Idaho.

With *skirmishes* with Native Americans mostly ended, mining boomed in Montana. In 1881, a significant share of the country's copper, gold, and silver came from Montana mines. Another industry that began to grow in the territory during the 1880s was cattle ranching.

As railroads connected the territory to the rest of the United States, Montana's population grew. Thousands of people—mostly German, Norwegian, and Swedish immigrants—migrated there to establish homesteads. They farmed and herded cattle in Montana.

Throughout the 1880s, Montana residents sought recognition as a U.S. state. Finally, on November 8, 1889, Montana was admitted as the 41st state. Helena became the capital.

Like many Western states, Montana was progressive with regard to women's rights. Women gained the right to vote in Montana elections in 1914, six years before passage of the Nineteenth Amendment to the U.S. *Constitution* granted that right to all American women. In 1916, Missoula native Jeannette M. Rankin became the first woman elected to the U.S. House of Representatives.

To improve farming, irrigation projects were implemented to divert water to farmland throughout the state. The construction of large *hydroelectric* dams on the Milk, Missouri, and Lower Yellowstone rivers provided electrical power to many of Montana's homes and businesses.

Farming in Montana was generally good until the 1920s, when a major drought killed crops and dried fertile soil. Many farmers sold their farms and looked for work in other states. Some moved to urban areas to look for work. Montana and North Dakota were the only two states in which the populations shrank during the 1920s.

Montana farmers continued to struggle during the 1930s, as the Great Depression took hold. More farms and banks closed. Lumber and mineral prices dropped. After being elected president in 1932, Franklin D. Roosevelt created programs to help states like Montana emerge from the Depression. Dams, bridges, and state parks were designated to improve the state infrastructure and put people to work. But the country did not emerge from the Depression until after the U.S. entered World War II in 1941.

Since the mid-20th century, there has been a shift in Montana from cattle ranching and logging to mining coal and drilling for oil and natural gas. Strip mining became the new technique for mining coal and other minerals. Massive strips of land are

Did You Know?

More gem-quality sapphires are produced in Montana than anywhere else in North America. A highly prized variety called the Yogo sapphire can be found only in Montana. Sapphires have been designated as one of Montana's official state gemstones.

unearthed, the minerals removed, and the land is buried again. This technique is controversial because it destroys good soil. An increase in coal production and exploration occurred in Montana in the 1970s.

Montana's oil and gas production have increased as well. The development of new methods to extract oil in the 2010s has led to an increase in oil production.

Government

The state of Montana is governed under a constitution that was ratified in 1972. This document replaced the state's original constitution from 1889. The state constitution defines the powers of the three branches of government—executive, legislative, and judicial—and outlines the rights of Montana's citizens.

The governor of Montana is head of the executive branch of state government. Governors are responsible for making sure that state laws are carried out, and do this by overseeing various state agencies and departments that engage in the day-to-day work of run-

ning the state. A lieutenant governor is the second-in-command, and takes office if the governor leaves or becomes unable to fulfill his duties. Both the governor and lieutenant governor are elected for four-year terms. The constitution prohibits these officers from serving more than eight years in a 16-year period. Other elect-

The Montana state capitol building in Helena. The statue depicts the first governor of the Montana Territory, Thomas F. Meagher.

ed state officials include the Secretary of State and Attorney General.

Like other states, Montana has a bicameral legislature. The state assembly includes 100 state representatives, while the state senate has 50 senators. The legislature only meets in odd-numbered years, and for 90-day periods. When they meet, legislators propose and vote on new laws. Representatives are not allowed to serve more than four two-year terms in office. Senators can serve no more than two four-year terms.

The judicial branch includes all legal courts in the state, which hear both civil and criminal cases. The highest court is the Montana Supreme Court, which hears cases related to the state government and interprets the meaning of state and local laws.

The Montana constitution includes a provision that voters may review their local form of government every ten years, and determine whether changes need to be made. This review is meant to ensure that the state and local governments are responsive to the concerns of residents.

The first woman to serve in Congress, Jeannette Rankin (1880–1973) was born in Missoula. She served a term in 1917–1918, but was not reelected. Rankin won a seat in Congress again in 1940 and served another two-year term.

Because of its low population, Montana has just one representative elected to the U.S. House of Representatives. Like all states, it has two U.S. Senators. In presidential elections, Montana has three votes in the electoral college.

The Economy

Agriculture, ranching, and forestry remain a significant part of Montana's economy. Large irrigated farms grow wheat, corn, canola, flaxseed, potatoes and sugar beets. The growing region is located in northeastern Montana.

The cattle region is found in northwestern Montana. Beef cattle are Montana's most important livestock product. Some of the country's biggest

Some Famous Montanans

A famous actor from the golden age of pictures was Gary Cooper (1901–1961). Known for his smooth style, Cooper starred in such movies as *A Farewell to Arms* (1932), *For Whom the Bell Tolls* (1943), and *High Noon* (1952).

Stunt man Robert "Evil" Knievel (1938–2007) was the epitome of an American daredevil. Born in Butte, Knievel became famous for his amazing and dangerous stunts during the 1960s and 1970s, such as using a motorcycle to jump over cars, busses, and even the Snake River Canyon in Idaho. He is in the Guinness Book of World Records for having broken more than 440 bones during his career.

Born in Missoula, actor and comedian Dana Carvey (b. 1955) is best known for his skits on *Saturday Night Live* and for starring in two *Wayne's World* movies.

Robert Yellowtail (1889–1988), a leader of the Crow Nation, was the first Native American to serve as superintendent of a reservation. He fought for the rights of the Crow Nation for many years.

Known for his paintings and bronze sculptures, Charles M. Russell (1864–1926) is considered one of the greatest artists of the American West. Russell came to Montana at age 16 to work on a ranch. In his studio at Great Falls, he would paint more than 2,000 works featuring cowboys, Native Americans, and the western landscape. Many of his works are on display in museums around the country, including the Charles M. Russell Museum Complex in Great Falls. A Russell painting titled "Lewis and Clark Meeting the Flathead Indians" hangs in the state capitol building in Helena.

Dana Carvey

"When Sioux and Blackfoot Meet,"
a painting by Charles M. Russell

A natural gas processing facility in Montana. The development of new technologies has led to greater production of oil and natural gas from shale formations in the state. The state also has four large oil refineries, located in Billings, Great Falls, and Laurel.

cattle ranches can be found in Montana. Dairy cattle, sheep, and hogs are also raised in the state.

The generation of hydroelectric power helps Montana's economy by reducing the price of electricity. Dams on rivers that flow from the Rocky Mountains produce 30 percent of Montana's electricity. Montana generates more electricity than it needs, and sells surplus power to nearby states like Wyoming and South Dakota.

Mining for coal, oil, and natural gas in western Montana has continued into the 21st century. Montana is the fifth-largest coal producer in the country. Most coal mining occurs in the Powder River Basin. Some Montana coal used to generate electricity, but most is shipped to power plants in nearby states.

In recent years, Montana's oil production has climbed due to new discoveries of oil, as well as new methods that make extracting the oil more feasible. A geological area known as the Bakken formation lies underneath Montana, North Dakota, and the Canadian provinces of Saskatchewan and Manitoba. The U.S. Geological Survey estimates that more than 7 billion barrels of oil could be extracted

At Great Falls, the Missouri River drops a total of 612 feet (187 m) from the top of the first falls to the bottom of the last. There are five hydroelectric dams on the river in this area, which generate electrical power for Montana homes and businesses.

from the rocky shale of Montana through a method known as fracking. However, this method is controversial because it can be very stressful for the environment.

Montana has four oil refineries, which take petroleum from the state or from nearby Canada and turn it into gasoline and other products. These refineries are a major industry in Montana. The state also has several facilities for processing natural gas.

Another industry is the timber industry, which is based in western Montana. The state supplies the coun-try with large amounts of wood prod-ucts. Minerals such as copper, gold, sapphires, and platinum are plentiful in the mountainous western part of the state.

Tourism is a growing industry in Montana. Tourists are drawn to the state for hunting and fishing, as well as to see spectacular scenery. In addi-tion to Glacier National Park and Yellowstone National Park, Montana has many state parks and wildlife refuges. The National Bison Range, the Charles M. Russell National Wildlife Refuge, and the Pine Butte

Swamp Preserve are also very popular among visitors.

The People

According to the U.S. Census Bureau, Montana's 2015 population is slightly more than 1 million residents. The majority of Montana residents (89 percent) are white, mostly of German or Scandinavian descent. In Montana cities and towns are generally located along irrigated valley bottoms.

About 66,000 Native Americans live in Montana, accounting for more than 6 percent of the population. Some Native Americans live on one of the seven reservations in Montana, but almost two-thirds of the Native Americans live in urban areas.

Montana residents appreciate their farming and cattle ranching heritage. They also respect the contributions and lifestyle of Native Americans, and education about native customs and cultures are mandated by state law for all students from kindergarten through twelfth grade. Many Montana residents enjoy the outdoor activities that their state has become famous for, such as hiking, camping, horse-

Aerial view of downtown Billings, the largest city in Montana.

back riding, and skiing. Montana is internationally known as a great place for hunting and fishing, and each year millions of tourists come to participate in these activities.

The Montana Institute of Arts and the Montana Arts Council fund dozens of state and local organizations that support the arts. These organizations provide many music, dance, literature, visual arts, folk life and arts and crafts events on an annual basis.

Major Cities

Helena, the capital of Montana, has a population of around 26,000, although another 50,000 people live in the suburbs nearby. Helena has a long mining history, and the land surrounding the city contain rich deposits of silver and lead. Mineral excavation and processing remain major industries there. Helena sits in a valley with a majestic view of the surrounding mountains.

The largest city in the state of Montana is ***Billings***. It is located in the south-central part of the state, on the Yellowstone River. According to the U.S. Census Bureau, Billings has a population of about 110,000 people. Billings has experienced rapid economic growth and its population has expanded over the past two decades. Much of the city's rapid growth is due to oil and shale mining outside of Billings. It is a center for trade and distribution of goods throughout Montana.

Missoula, located in western Montana near the Idaho border, has a population of about 70,000, according to recent U.S. Census Bureau estimates. Missoula is surrounded by steep hills and rocky terrain. The University of Montana is located in Missoula.

Montana's third-largest city, ***Great Falls***, takes its name from a series of five nearby waterfalls on Missouri River. Today, hydroelectric dams operate at each of the falls, leading to the nickname "the Electric City." Malmstrom Air Force Base is located in Great Falls, as is Montana State University and several smaller colleges. Great Falls has a population of about 60,000.

Further Reading

Bailer, Darice. *What's Great About Montana*. Minneapolis: Lerner Publications, 2014.

Jewell, Judy, and Bill McRea. *Discover Montana*. Berkeley, Calif.: Avalon Travel, 2012.

Therriault, Ednor. *Montana Curiosities: Quirky Characters, Roadside Oddities & Other Offbeat Stuff*. Guilford, Conn.: Globe Pequot, 2010.

Internet Resources

www.infoplease.com/us-states/montana.html

This site contains interesting facts about Montana.

http://quickfacts.census.gov/qfd/states/30000.html

This U.S. Census Bureau web page contains all kinds of information about the state of Montana and its people.

http://dnrc.mt.gov/forestry

This is the state government site for Montana's forest and wildlife information.

 Text-Dependent Questions

1. What are two reasons for population growth in Montana during the 19th century?
2. Who was the first woman elected to the U.S. Congress
3. What is the name of the geological formation that is thought to contain more than 7 billion barrels of oil?

Research Project

Design a western mining town in Montana in the middle of the 19th century. Good examples are Virginia City and Bannak. Do this through drawing or creating the town by using materials of choice. Explain your project to your class.

North Dakota at a Glance

Area: 70,698 sq mi (183,107 sq km)[1].
  19th largest state
  Land: 68,994 sq mi (178,694 sq km)
  Water: 1,710 sq mi (4,429 sq km)
Highest elevation: White Butte, 3,506
  feet (1,069 m)
Lowest elevation: Red River in
  Pembina County, 750 feet (229 m)

Statehood: November 2, 1889
  (39th state)

Capital: Bismarck

Population: 739,482 (47th)[2]

State nickname: Flickertail State,
  Peace Garden State
State bird: western meadowlark
State flower: wild prairie rose

[1] *U.S. Census Bureau*
[2] *U.S. Census Bureau, 2014 estimate*

North Dakota

If asked the question, "what is North Dakota like?," many people would probably say, "cold, flat, and lonely." These three adjectives certainly describe North Dakota in some ways: the weather can be cold; the state is mostly flat; and it is one of the least densely populated states in the U.S., with just 10.5 people per square mile (4.0 per sq km). However, North Dakota has much more to offer than that description implies.

Geography

North Dakota is located in the north-central United States. Minnesota borders the state to the east. South Dakota, obviously, is to the south. It borders Montana to the west, and shares a northern border with the Canadian provinces of Manitoba and Saskatchewan. As the nineteenth-largest state in the country by area, North Dakota covers 70,698 square miles (183,107 square kilometers).

North Dakota can be divided into three geographic regions. In the eastern part of the state, the Red River Valley is flat and has rich, fertile soil, making it ideal for farming. This region is the state's leading producer of agricultural products like canola, flaxseed, sunflower oil, various beans, wheat, and honey.

To the west of the Red River Valley is a region known as the Drift Prairie. It's located in the center of the state. The Drift Prairie region's low, rolling hills and shallow lakes were formed by the movement of glaciers thousands of years ago. The Missouri Plateau is the name given to a large plateau that stretches to the east of the Missouri River. The Missouri is North Dakota's largest river, and flows through the state into South Dakota.

To the west of the Missouri River lies another plateau. This region, known as the Great Plains, is covered with grassy hills that seem to extend forever. This region receives less precipitation than the rest of the state. Herds of cattle, as well as wild animals like bison, graze in this grass-covered area. *Lignite coal* and petroleum are major natural resources that are found in the western part of the state.

The Badlands are an unusual geological formation in southwestern North Dakota. The region was named by French fur traders because of the harsh traveling conditions found there. The Badlands consists of deep,

 # Words to Understand in This Chapter

butte—an isolated hill with extremely steep sides and a flat top.

lignite coal—a type of combustible sedimentary rock that is formed from decaying plant material over millions of years. When burned, lignite coal does not produce as much heat as bituminous or anthracite coal.

nomadic—roaming from place to place instead of remaining fixed to a geographic location.

colorful canyons formed by erosion. This region, which stretches into South Dakota, contains many sharp cliffs and **buttes**.

The climate in North Dakota can be extreme. The highest recorded temperature is above 121 degrees Fahrenheit and the lowest is into the -60's below zero. The summers are short and the winters are cold and long.

Typically, the state experiences short, mild summers and longer, cold winters. The average summer temperature in northern North Dakota is around 82°F (29°C). Winter sets in

The Little Missouri River, a 560-mile-long (901-km-long) tributary of the Missouri River, flows through Theodore Roosevelt National Park in North Dakota.

during October and lasts until April, with average temperatures between 30°F and –5°F (–1°C and –21°C). It has snowed in North Dakota during every month except June and July.

The average rainfall in North Dakota is roughly 17 inches per year. This is about half of the national average rainfall. The state has periodically suffered from extreme dry periods. At the same time, heavy snowmelt sometimes causes flooding along the Missouri and Red rivers. In 2009, many North Dakota communities, including Fargo and Grand Forks, suffered from massive flooding.

Fargo is typically covered in snow during the winter months. The city typically receives about 50 inches (127 cm) of snow every winter.

History

More than 12,000 years ago, Paleo-Indians crossed the Bering Strait land mass that once connected Asia to North America. These early Indians were *nomadic*. They followed herds of bison, lived in tepees made from bison skin and fur, and dug earth-covered homes that sheltered them from bad weather. Over time they migrated through Canada and into what today is North Dakota.

By the time the first Europeans arrived in this part of North America during the 18th century, there were a number of Native American tribes living in the region. These included the Mandan and Hidatsa tribes, which living along the Missouri River. The Arikara, Cheyenne, and Sioux tribes also lived in the region.

The French claimed the vast wilderness of North America during the seventeenth century. The first French explorer to enter the area today known as North Dakota was Pierre Gaultier de Varennes, sieur de La Vérendrye. In 1738, La Vérendrye led an expedition from Canada (then called New France) in search of a water route to the Pacific Ocean. He discovered a village of Mandan

This 19th-century illustration by the respected artist Karl Bodmer shows a group of Mandan warriors performing a ritual dance to ensure a good buffalo hunt. The Mandan lived in North and South Dakota along the Missouri River, and engaged peacefully with both French fur traders and later with American settlers in the region.

Native American tepees are set up outside Fort Union, which from 1828 to 1867 was the most important fur trade post on the Upper Missouri River. The tribes of the Northern Plains, including the Mandan, Hidatsa, Sioux, Cheyenne, and Arikara, often visited the outpost to exchange buffalo robes and furs for manufactured goods such as cloth, guns, blankets, and beads. The fort is now a national historic site.

Indians and stayed with them for a brief time. La Vérendrye's sons also explored the region during the 1740s.

Unlike the nomadic Native American tribes of the region, the Mandan lived in villages year-round. This made them ideal partners for trade with French fur trappers and traders. However, this contact with Europeans had a devastating effect on the Native Americans. Whites carried a deadly disease called smallpox, for which the natives had no natural immunity or resistance. In the 1780s, smallpox devastated the Mandan peo-ple. Thousands died, and entire villages were left uninhabited. The Hidatsa, Arikara, and Cheyenne people were also affected by smallpox outbreaks.

In 1803, the French government agreed to sell its North American territory to the United States. After making the Louisiana Purchase, U.S. President Thomas Jefferson sent Meriwether Lewis and William Clark to explore and map this wild region. Their journey began in May 1804, when their party of about 40 soldiers and guides left St. Louis, travelling west on the Missouri River. Lewis and Clark spent the winter of 1804-05 at an outpost they called Fort Mandan, near the modern-day town of Washburn. They eventually reached the Pacific Ocean, and returned to St. Louis in 1806.

By this time, the first European settlements had been established in North Dakota. In 1801, Alexander Henry established a trading post at Pembina. In 1802, John Cameron built a trading post at the current site of Grand Forks.

During the first half of the 19th century, white settlers began trickling into the Upper Plains region. In the 1820s, the border between the United States and Canada was established north of Pembina. During the 1830s and 1840s, fur trading posts were established throughout the region.

In 1861 the federal government established the Dakota Territory, which included both North and South Dakota. White settlers continued to slowly move into the territory as the government offered free land to people willing to establish homesteads there. Most of these were of immigrants of German, Norwegian, Scot-Irish, English, and Swedish descent.

Fort Buford was a U.S. Army post established in 1866 where the Missouri and Yellowstone Rivers meet. The U.S. military used forts like this to protect settlers in the Dakota Territory. Most of the fort's buildings were destroyed when the fort was closed in the 1890s. Today, the North Dakota State Historical Society operates the Fort Buford State Historic Site.

President Theodore Roosevelt speaks to a crowd of children in Mandan, 1903. The 26th president had lived in North Dakota during the 1880s, where he was a cattle rancher until the severe winter of 1886–1887 wiped out his herd.

They were mostly farmers and ranchers and some miners. Railroads connected farmers to markets for their crops in the eastern states.

As the population of the Dakota Territory increased, the push for statehood grew. On November 2, 1889, President Benjamin Harrison signed a bill dividing the territory into two new states, North and South Dakota.

North Dakota became the 39th state, while South Dakota was considered the 40th state.

The early 20th century was an up-and-down economic period, especially for farmers in North Dakota. In the late 1910s and early 1920s, farmers earned great money growing wheat and other crops, due to good weather and the demand for food caused by World War I in Europe. Crops like sugar beets and potatoes were also profitable. New farmers moved into the state, and the population of North Dakota increased to 680,845 people by 1930.

When the Great Depression began in the late 1920s, North Dakotans were hit very hard. An unfortunate mix of drought and plummeting crop prices forced many North Dakotan farmers out of business. One-third of the state's farmers lost their land. North Dakota was the poorest state in the country during the Depression, and by 1940 nearly 40,000 residents (more than 6 percent of the population) had moved to other states seeking work.

The United States entered World War II in 1941. This was a benefit to North Dakota farmers, who saw profits again by providing food for the troops fighting overseas.

In 1944, the U.S. Congress passed legislation intended to control the use of water from the Missouri River. The Pick–Sloan Missouri Basin Program, as it became known, was intended to prevent flooding, divert water for irrigation of agricultural fields, and use water power to generate electricity. To accomplish these goals, a series of dams were built on the Missouri River during the 1940s and 1950s. In North Dakota, the Garrison Dam was completed in 1954. Today, this hydroelectric dam continues to provide power to most of North Dakota.

Although the project brought benefits to North Dakota, it was not without controversy. Construction of the dam created a huge manmade lake, Lake Sakakawea, that submerged what had been a reservation for the Mandan, Hidatsa, and Arikara tribes (now known as the Three Affiliated Nations). Despite their protests, the land was taken. Some of the Native Americans had to be forcibly removed from their homes.

In early 2009, practically the entire state of North Dakota experienced significant flooding. The floods were caused when unusually heavy winter snows melted in March. This photo shows the Red River flooding the Sorlie Bridge in Grand Forks.

An oil rig in the Williston basin, a region of North Dakota with rich deposits of oil, natural gas, and lignite coal.

In March 1966, North Dakota was hit with one of the worst blizzards in the state's history. The storm dumped roughly three feet of snow in some parts of the state, and the prairie winds created snowdrifts that were up to 20 feet deep and hundreds of feet long. Five people, and nearly 140,000 head of livestock, perished in the storm. When the snow eventually melted, it contributed to flooding of the Red River that caused additional damage.

Oil was discovered in North Dakota during the 1950s, but it was not fully exploited until the U.S. experienced an oil crisis in the 1970s. During the late 1970s, oil drilling and refining in North Dakota created thousands of new jobs. However, by the mid-1980s the international price of oil had fallen below the level where it was economical to extract oil from the Williston Basin in North Dakota, and the boom ended.

Beginning around 2006, however, new techniques were developed that made it economically feasible to remove oil from an underground geological feature known as the Bakken Formation. As a result, North Dakota has experienced a second oil boom, one that has resulted in enough jobs to give North Dakota the lowest unemployment rate in the United States by 2011. By 2012, North Dakota had moved to second among U.S. states with regard to oil production, behind only Texas. Revenue from oil has helped to fund many new government programs in the state.

North Dakota's state capitol building in Bismarck includes a 19-story tower. It is the tallest building in the state.

Government

North Dakota's original constitution was ratified in 1889, but it has been amended several times since then. Like other states, the government of North Dakota has three branches: executive, legislative, and judicial.

A governor and lieutenant governor lead the executive branch of North Dakota's state government. Governors and lieutenant governors are elected to four-year terms.

North Dakota is unusual in that the leaders of many executive depart-

Famous People from North Dakota

Basketball coach Phil Jackson (b. 1945) attended high school in Williston and college at the University of North Dakota. Considered one of the greatest basketball coaches of all time, he won 11 NBA titles with the Chicago Bulls and Los Angeles Lakers.

Phil Jackson

Author Louis L'Amour (1908–1988), born in Jamestown, wrote more than 100 novels and short stories about cowboys and the American West. He is considered the all-time best-selling writer of Westerns, with total sales of more than 200 million copies.

Baseball player Roger Maris, (1934–1985) played in the major leagues from 1957 to 1968. In 1961, he hit 61 home runs for the New York Yankees, breaking the record of 60 that had been set in 1927 by Babe Ruth.

Entertainer Lawrence Welk (1903–1992) hosted a popular television variety show, featuring music and dancing, that aired from 1951 to 1982. Welk lived on the family farm in Strasburg until he was 21, when he left to pursue his music career. *The Lawrence Welk Show* can still be seen in reruns on PBS stations.

Clifford "Fido" Purpur (1914–2001) born in Grand Forks, is recognized as the first North Dakotan to play in the National Hockey League (NHL). Clifford played for the St. Louis Eagles, Chicago Blackhawks, and Detroit Red Wings. He was inducted into the U.S. Hockey Hall of Fame in 1974.

Josh Duhamel (b. 1972) was born in Minot and played football at Minot State University before launching an acting career. He has appeared in many television shows, including *All My Children* and *Vegas*, and starred in three *Transformers* films.

Josh Duhamel

Sacagawea (c.1788–1812?) was the daughter of a Shoshone chief. After being captured by an enemy tribe, she was married to a French Canadian trapper. They lived along the Upper Missouri River with the Hidatsa and Mandan Indians in what would become North Dakota. She was a very useful guide and interpreter for William Clark and Meriwether Lewis during their 1804–1806 exploration of the Louisiana Purchase.

ments are elected by statewide vote, rather than appointed by the governor. The 13 elected executive positions include Attorney General, Auditor, Treasurer, Insurance Commissioner, Superintendent of Public Instruction, and Agriculture Commissioner. All of these officers are elected to four-year terms.

Agriculture Commissioner is a high-profile office in North Dakota, because of the importance of farming in the state. The Agriculture Commissioner serves with the governor and Attorney General on the three-member North Dakota

Industrial Commission, which oversees several state-owned enterprises. These include grain elevators, banks, and programs for developing and leasing the state's natural resources, such as coal, minerals, and oil.

North Dakota's legislature is bicameral, consisting of a Senate and House of Representatives. The state is divided into 47 districts, and each elects one senator (for a total of 47) and two representatives (for a total of 94) to the state legislature. Legislators in both houses are elected to four-year terms. The assembly holds sessions in every odd-numbered year, unless a

The North Dakota House of Representatives meets in this chamber in the state capitol building.

Cattle graze on a North Dakota ranch. There are approximately three times as many cattle as people living in the state.

special session is called by the governor.

The highest court in North Dakota is the state Supreme Court, which includes five justices. North Dakota also has a system of state courts that handle both criminal and civil matters.

North Dakota is represented in the federal government by two senators and one representative. In presidential elections, the candidate who wins the most popular votes in North Dakota receives three electoral votes.

The Economy

Agriculture dominates in North Dakota. The Red River Valley contains some of the finest agricultural soil in the world. Nearly 90 percent of North Dakota's land area is used for farms and ranches.

One quarter of North Dakota's economic production is related to agriculture. Currently, revenue from crops and the sale of livestock totals nearly $6 billion a year. Among other crops, North Dakota is a top producer of honey, easily doubling the amount produced in any other U.S. state.

A quarter of North Dakota's work force is in farm production or farm and ranching related jobs. North Dakota has just over 30,000 farms and ranches. The average size farm is 1,240 acres.

The state has other resources as

A high-clearance sprayer irrigates a farm field.

well. A massive quantity of lignite coal is in the northwestern part of the state. Power plants use lignite coal. These plants produce electricity for most of North Dakota and some of the Midwest.

Windmills in North Dakota produce more wind-generated electricity than any other state in the United States.

Only Texas, Alaska, and California produce more oil than North Dakota. The counties that produce the most oil are Williams, Billings, Mountrail, Dunn, Bowman, and McKenzie. Only one county (Trail County) in the entire state has not had some kind of oil and natural gas drilling or exploration.

The business climate is improving in North Dakota. A little over 27 percent of the workforce has a bachelor's degree or higher, and more than half of the residents are employed outside the farm industry. Nearly 50,000 students study in North Dakota.

The People

According to U.S. Census Bureau, the population of North Dakota was about 740,000 by 2015.

As in the other states of the Upper Plains region, most residents of North Dakota are from a Western European or Scandinavian background. Whites make up roughly 90 percent of the population, with Native Americans accounting for 5.4 percent. There are very few African Americans (1.8 percent), Asians (1.2 percent), or Hispanics (2.9 percent). More than 94 percent of the state's residents speak English at home.

Overall, the income level for adults is very close to the national average. According to the Census Bureau, the

North Dakota produces more sunflowers than any other state.

The Chateau de Mores, a 26-room, two-story frame building, was built in 1883 as the summer residence of the Marquis de Mores, a French nobleman who operated a ranch in North Dakota. The Chateau, located near Medora, now houses a museum run by the state historical society.

average income of a North Dakota resident (adjusted for 2013 dollars) is $29,732. The national average is $28,155. However, the median household income in the state is $53,741, slightly higher than the national average of $53,046. About 12 percent of North Dakota residents live below the federal poverty level, compared to 15.4 percent of all Americans.

The people of North Dakota consider themselves to be rugged and independent, due in part to the state's farming heritage and to the extreme weather that the state experiences. and its higher percentage of outdoor-related occupations.

Major Cities

Fargo is the largest city in North Dakota, with a population of just over 200,000 residents. It is near the Red River Valley. Fargo has a symphony, and is home to the Red River Zoo, the Plain Arts Museum, a medical center, and North Dakota State University.

According to the U.S. Census Bureau, *Bismarck* has a population of about 95,000 residents. Lewis and Clark passed through the area occu-

Aerial view of Grand Forks, North Dakota's third-largest city. Across the Red River is the sister city of East Grand Forks, a separate municipality with a population of about 9,000.

pied by the city during their travels through the Louisiana Purchase in the early 1800s. Bismarck has been the state's capitol since 1893. Previously, the capital was in **Yankton**. The state capitol building, governor's mansion, and a historical museum share the same site in downtown Bismarck.

Located where the Red River and the Red Lakes River meet, **Grand Forks** is the third-largest city in North Dakota, with nearly 55,000 residents. Grand Forks is well located for soil cultivation and is an important ecomomic center in the state. Currently, Grand Forks is home to manufacturing facilities, food processing firms, and sites for scientific research.

Further Reading

National Geographic Kids World Atlas. Washington, D.C.: National Geographic Children's Books, 2012.

Redmond, Jim, and D.J. Ross. *Uniquely North Dakota*. Chicago: Heinemann Library, 2004.

Watson, Galadriel Findlay. *North Dakota: The Peace Garden State*. New York: Weigl Publishing), 2011.

Internet Resources

http://history.nd.gov/ndhistory/settlement.html

The website of the Historical Society of North Dakota provides articles and photos related to North Dakota's history.

http://www.nrcs.usda.gov/wps/portal/nrcs/site/nd/home

Official web page of the U.S. Department of Agriculture's Natural Resources Conservation Service for North Dakota.

http://www.ndstudies.org/resources/legendary/quick-facts.html

The state government provides information about the North Dakota Education Studies Project at this website.

 # Text-Dependent Questions

1. In which part of North Dakota do most cattle ranchers live?
2. What is the purpose of the North Dakota Industrial Commission?

Research Project

Do some research about the life of a cattle rancher in North Dakota. Write a one-page journal entry that records a typical day in a rancher's. Use specific details found in your research in your journal entry.

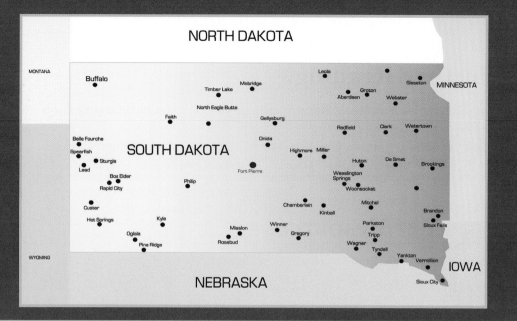

South Dakota at a Glance

Area: 77,116 sq mi (199,729 sq km)[1].
  17th largest state
  Land: 75,811 sq mi (196,350 sq km)
  Water: 1305 sq mi (3,379 sq km)
Highest elevation: Harney Peak,
  7,242 feet (2,207 m)
Lowest elevation: Big Stone Lake, 966
  feet (294 m) below sea level

Statehood: November 2, 1889
  (39th state)

Capital: Pierre

Population: 844,877 (46th)[2]

State nickname: the Monument State
State bird: ring-necked pheasant
State flower: American pasqueflower

[1] U.S. Census Bureau
[2] U.S. Census Bureau, 2014 estimate

South Dakota

South Dakota is best known today for its pristine national parks and for internationally famous monuments such as Mount Rushmore. But the state has played an important role in American history.

Geography

Unlike many U.S. states, the shape of South Dakota is basic and geometric: it is a 77,116 square mile (199,729 sq km) rectangle. South Dakota is the 14th-largest state. It borders North Dakota to the north, Nebraska to the south, Minnesota and Iowa to the east, and Wyoming and Montana to the west.

The Missouri River divides South Dakota into two regions. The two regions are known to residents as East River and West River. East River is more heavily populated, and includes the state's largest city, Sioux Falls. This area receives more precipitation, and its flatter terrain is ideal for farming. West River is *arid* and contains rugged terrain; cattle ranching is more common in this area. The largest community in West River is Rapid City; this region also includes such tourist attractions as Mount Rushmore and the Badlands.

Millions of years of erosion, as well as glacier activity, formed the terrain of South Dakota. West of the Little Missouri River, flat and grassy prairies known as the Great Plains stretch into South Dakota. Tall buttes dot a tan and dry landscape in the southwestern part of South Dakota. High rocky canyons meet expanses of flat lands. This section of the Great Plains features a colorful area known as the Badlands. This region runs along the Cheyenne River and is about 100 miles (161 km) long.

The Missouri Plateau extends into South Dakota. This is the center of the state and the flattest part of South Dakota. Most of South Dakota's farms are located on this plateau.

The Black Hills are located in the western part of the state and rise some 3,000 feet (914 m) higher than the surrounding terrain. This region got its name from the darkness captured by its deep river valleys. These valleys cast a dark appearance over the entire land that is the Black Hills. The Sioux tribe has long considered the Black Hills to be *sacred* land. Nearly two-thirds of the Black Hills are located in South Dakota. The remainder are in Wyoming.

Harney Peak, located in the Black Hills, is the highest point of the eastern Rocky Mountains, rising 7,242 feet (2,207 m) It is located 10 miles

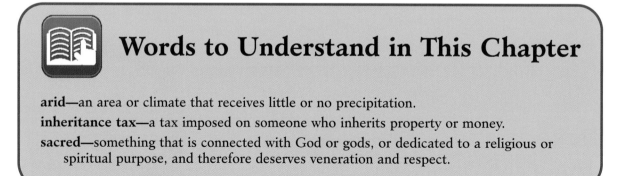

📖 Words to Understand in This Chapter

arid—an area or climate that receives little or no precipitation.
inheritance tax—a tax imposed on someone who inherits property or money.
sacred—something that is connected with God or gods, or dedicated to a religious or spiritual purpose, and therefore deserves veneration and respect.

Scenic view of Badlands National Park. The colorful formations were formed by 500,000 years of erosion, and hold the fossil remains of creatures from millions of years ago.

Granite outcroppings and woods surround a lake in the Black Hills.

A corn field stands near an ethanol production plant on the Missouri River. In 2014, South Dakota ranked fifth among all U.S. states in production of ethanol, a biofuel made from corn and other grains that is often added to fuels like diesel and gasoline to reduce carbon monoxide and other emissions.

(16 km) north of Mount Rushmore National Memorial.

Most of South Dakota's forested land is found in the Black Hills National Forest or in Custer State Park. Many animals live in these areas, including antelope, elk, beaver, bobcats, porcupines, coyotes, and cottontail rabbits. Just as in North Dakota, concentrations of prairie dogs can also be found in South Dakota.

The climate in South Dakota is similar to North Dakota. Extreme temperatures sometimes occur, with temperatures as low as –40°F (–40°C) in winter or as high as 115°F (46°C) in summer. Generally, the temperature ranges from 0°F (–17°C) in the coldest winter months to around 86°F (30°C) in the summer months. On average, South Dakota receives 20 inches (51 cm) of rainfall per year. The eastern part of the state receives a little more precipitation than the western part of the state.

History

Like other states in this region, South Dakota was originally settled by Paleo-Indians who had traveled from Asia into North America on the land bridge that once connected Alaska and Russia. Over thousands of years, Native American cultures developed and changed. By the early 19th century, the land was inhabited by the Mandan, Arikara, Omaha, Ponca and Sioux tribes.

The first white explorers in this region arrived during the late 17th century. One of them was the Frenchman Rene-Robert Cavelier, Sieur de La Salle, who claimed the area for France. South Dakota was part of the vast Louisiana Territory, which France sold to the United States in 1803.

Americans were slow to settle in the Dakota Territory. During the 1820s and 1830s, a few hardy fur trappers and traders explored the region. It was not until the 1850s that white settlers began to arrive in the land in larger numbers, intending to establish farms and built permanent settlements. The U.S. Army established Fort Randall in 1856 in order to make sure there was peace on the frontier between whites and Native Americans. That same year, the city of Sioux Falls was founded.

Did You Know?

The South Dakota Badlands are known as the "playground of the dinosaurs," because dinosaur bones from millions of years ago have been found there. In 1990, the best-preserved Tyrannosaurus Rex skeleton was discovered in the Badlands. The remains of other long-extinct animals, such as a dog-sized camel and a three-toed horse, have also been found in Badlands National Park.

In a series of treaties, the Sioux agreed to allow whites to settle in the southern part of South Dakota. According to the Fort Laramie Treaty of 1868, the northern region, including the sacred Black Hills, was supposed to be Sioux territory forever.

It would not be long before this promise would be broken. During the early 1870s, a newly completed railroad brought many new settlers to South Dakota. In 1874, as white settlement expanded, Lieutenant Colonel George A. Custer led a mili-

Lieutenant Colonel George A. Custer underestimated the strength of a Native American force he attacked near the Little Bighorn River, and the Sioux and Cheyenne warriors crushed the U.S. Seventh Cavalry in July 1876.

tary expedition to the southern part of the Dakota Territory. When Custer reported that gold had been found in the Black Hills, thousands of gold seekers flocked there. They illegally established towns like Deadwood, where there were few laws and miners could get the supplies they needed.

Over the next few years, the U.S. Army was unable to keep miners out of the Black Hills. In 1876, the Sioux and Cheyenne tribes went to war to defend their territory from this inva-

sion. Among the best known leaders were the warrior Crazy Horse and the chief Sitting Bull.

The Native Americans won some of the clashes that occurred between 1876 and 1877. Their most famous victory came in June 1876 at the Battle of the Little Bighorn in South Dakota, when a force of 700 soldiers under Custer were wiped out by a much larger band of Sioux warriors. But over time the Americans' superior weapons and greater numbers eventually forced the Native Americans to end the war and accept living on reservations.

In the late 1870s and 1880s, the largest city in South Dakota was Lead, because of the Homestake Gold Mine. The Homestake Mine soon became the world's largest gold mine.

The white population of South Dakota swelled from about 80,000 in 1878 to well over 300,000 in 1888. Railroads continued to spread into the Dakota Territory, and more gold-mining towns developed. As the population of the southern part of the Dakota Territory grew, there was a movement for statehood. On November 2, 1889, South Dakota became the 40th official U.S. state.

In December 1890, the last major clash of the frontier wars between Native Americans and the U.S. Army occurred in South Dakota. Starving because they had not received food promised to them by the U.S. government, a band of Teton Sioux led by chief Spotted Elk left their reservation. When American soldiers caught up to them at Wounded Knee Creek, they massacred many of the Native Americans. More than 150 Sioux men, women, and children were killed.

During the early 20th century, immigrants continued to arrive in South Dakota. These settlers were mostly German, Irish, or Scandinavian. Many were farmers or ranchers, growing wheat and raising cattle.

When the Great Depression hit in the early 1930s. South Dakota farmers were battered by a devastating combination of drought and plummeting crop prices. The drought was especially harsh in South Dakota. The lack of rain turned the once-fertile soil to

South Dakota farmers pose with a steam tractor, 1907. The methods used to plow the prairies caused soil erosion, leading to the Midwestern "Dust Bowl" of the 1930s.

gritty dust, which could be picked up by strong winds and blown into blinding dust storms. In 1931, adding to this misery, hordes of grasshoppers descended on South Dakota fields and ate any crops worth harvesting during this time.

Some farmers ended up moving to urban areas looking for different work. Others left the state altogether. South Dakota's population declined by more than 7 percent between 1930 and 1940.

After the United States entered World War II in 1941, South Dakota

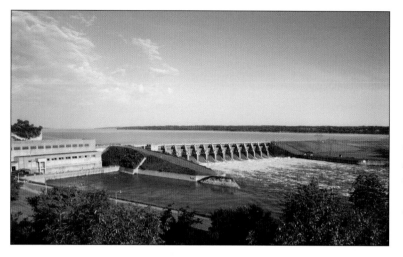

Gavins Point Dam is a hydroelectric dam on the Missouri River at the point where it exits South Dakota and enters Nebraska. It was built in the 1950s as part of the Pick-Sloan Missouri Basin Program, which proposed a series of dams to control flooding and generate hydroelectric power. The large body of water behind the dam is Lewis and Clark Lake, which draws approximately one million visitors a year for recreational activities.

farmers saw some improvement. The state helped to provide food for the troops and also contributed several thousand soldiers to fight in the war.

During the 1940s, a project to control the Missouri River and harness its power began to be implemented. Over the next thirty years, many dams were built in South Dakota to control flooding, provide water for crop irrigation, and generate hydroelectric power. Gigantic lakes formed behind these dams, and tourists soon realized that these lakes were excellent for fishing and other vacation activities.

In June 1972, heavy rain caused the Canyon Lake Dam to collapse. Floodwaters washed through nearby Rapid City, killing 238 people, injuring thousands more, and destroying more than 1,300 homes. It was one of the worst disasters in South Dakota history.

The 1990s brought some economic relief to South Dakota through tourism and as well as the construction of casinos on Native American reservations.

Today, farming remains the primary economic activity in South Dakota. However, tourism is very important. Visitors to Mount

Rushmore or other national parks and Native American sites provide a significant source of revenue to state businesses.

Government

Like most states, the government of South Dakota consists of three official branches: executive, legislative, and judicial. South Dakota is governed under its original constitution, ratified in 1889, although that document has been amended several times over the years.

A governor, elected for a four-year term, heads the executive branch of the state government. Governors can serve a maximum of two terms. The governor appoints some state officers, as well as the heads of state agencies who make sure that the laws are obeyed within South Dakota. The governor can call for special sessions of the state legislature, and must either approve or veto all new laws passed by the legislature.

South Dakota has a bicameral, or two-part, legislature. The state Senate contains 35 senators, while the state House of Representatives contains 70 representatives. The legislature passes laws and raises taxes to make sure the

The grounds of the South Dakota state capitol building in Pierre are quite beautiful. The building overlooks the Missouri River. Scenic trails with statues, a sparkling lake, and a manicured garden share the property.

laws are carried out.

The judicial branch is the legal part of the government. The highest court in South Dakota is the state Supreme Court. There are five justices on South Dakota's Supreme Court. Lower courts serve counties and townships.

South Dakota is divided into 66 counties. Within the countries are more than a thousand smaller municipalities, called townships, as well as larger cities. The state capital is Pierre.

Because of its relatively small population, South Dakota is represented in the U.S. House of Representatives by one legislator. Like all states, South Dakota has two U.S. Senators. In presidential elections, the state has three votes in the Electoral College.

The Economy

South Dakota's economy is based on agriculture, tourism, and forestry. The state remains a leading producer of corn, canola, rye, flaxseed, wheat, and soybeans. The southern part of the state is excellent for raising and herding livestock. South Dakota has been among the nation's leading cattle pro-

ducers since the early 20th century. It's a major producer of wool as well. Timber harvesting is an important industry in the Black Hills area.

Sites like Mount Rushmore draw millions of people to the state each year, generating much revenue. The colossal monument to presidents George Washington, Thomas Jefferson, Abraham Lincoln, and Theodore Roosevelt are carved into two square miles (5 sq km) of granite, and rise 5,720 feet (1,743 m) above the landscape. Each of the stone heads is 60 feet (18 m) tall.

Mount Rushmore is not the only monument in the Black Hills. A memorial to the Sioux leader Crazy Horse is being carved out of granite atop Mount Thunderhead. It took nearly 40 years of work before the face of Crazy Horse was completed in 1998. Work on the rest of the figure is ongoing.

South Dakota also has some of the country's finest state parks, as well as pristine lakes surrounded by wildlife. These attract visitors from all over who enjoy nature and outdoor pursuits like hiking, fishing, hunting, and camping.

South Dakota is considered to have a favorable climate for businesses. One of the nation's largest banking and credit card firms, Citibank, has its headquarters in Sioux Falls. Other financial firms based in the state include Wells Fargo, Capital One, and First Premier Bank.

Mining for natural resources, such as gold, continue in South Dakota. The Homestake Mine was the world's largest gold mine until it closed in 2001. Stone and sand are quarried to make cement. A small amount of oil is also extracted from beneath the ground in South Dakota.

The U.S. military has a significant presence in South Dakota. Ellsworth Air Force Base is one of the state's largest employers, providing some 4,500 jobs.

During the Cold War (1949–1992), nuclear missile silos were hidden in South Dakota near Ellsworth AFB. In 1999, Minuteman Missile National Historic Site was established to pre-

A variety of munitions are lined up on the flightline near parked B-1B Lancer bombers at Ellsworth Air Force Base. The base is home to the U.S. Air Force's 28th Bomb Wing, which in recent years has been involved in combat bombing missions in Iraq and Afghanistan.

Some Famous South Dakotans

Former television newscaster Tom Brokaw (b. 1940) was born in Webster and graduated from the University of South Dakota. He was anchor of *NBC Nightly News* from 1982 to 2004 and wrote the bestselling book *The Greatest Generation*.

Tom Daschle (b. 1947) represented South Dakota in the U.S. Congress for many years, serving in the House of Representatives from 1979 until 1987, and in the U.S. Senate from 1987 until 2005. He was the Senate's Democratic Party leader from 1995 until 2005.

The Native American activist Russell Means (1939–2012) was a member of the Oglala Sioux tribe, born in Shannon. During the 1960s he became a leader of the American Indian Movement (AIM), and helped organize several notable events by that organization, including the 1973 occupation of Wounded Knee. Means lived on the Pine Ridge Indian Reservation in South Dakota.

Russell Means

Author Laura Ingalls Wilder (1867–1957) moved with her family to DeSmet when she was a teenager. She would later write about her life in a pioneer family in an acclaimed series of books for children. *The Long Winter* (1940), her sixth book, tells how her family survived the severe winter of 1880–1881 in DeSmet.

At the 1964 Olympics, Billy Mills (b. 1938) became the second Native American to win an Olympic gold medal. A member of the Sioux tribe, Mills won the 10,000 meter race, setting an Olympic record in the process.

Other notable athletes have ties to South Dakota. Placekicker Adam Vinatieri (b. 1972) was born in Yankton and played football at South Dakota State University. In the NFL, he was the kicker for four Super Bowl–winning teams, and holds the NFL record for career postseason field goals. UFC fighter Broc Lesnar (b. 1977) grew up on a dairy farm in Webster. Former WNBA basketball player Becky Hammon (b. 1977) grew up in Rapid City. After her professional basketball career ended, in 2014 Hammon became the first woman to hold a full-time coaching position in the NBA.

Becky Hammon

serve two 1960s-era Intercontinental Ballistic Missile (ICBM) sites.

The People

According to the U.S. Census Bureau, the total population of South Dakota is about 845,000. Roughly 85 percent of the residents of this state are white. People of German descent make up the largest ethnic group in South Dakota, followed by Irish Americans and Scandinavian Americans.

South Dakota has the largest Native American population in the country, at about 66,000 people, representing about 8.5 percent of the state's total population. The state is home to nine reservations, where about half of the state's Native Americans live. Unfortunately, conditions on South Dakota's reservations are often poor. Native Americans suffer from a lack of jobs, as well as inadequate healthcare and educational opportunities.

In 1973, about 200 armed members of the American Indian Movement (AIM) occupied the small town of Wounded Knee to protest government policies. They held out for 71 days, while the federal and state authorities surrounded the town. The incident at Wounded Knee attracted national attention to the plight of Native Americans.

According to the Census Bureau, the average South Dakota resident makes less money than the average American citizen. The average income for a South Dakotan was about $25,740 in 2014, which is a few thousand dollars below the national average of $28,155. However, the percentage of South Dakotans living below the federal poverty level (14.1 percent) is lower than the national average (15.4 percent).

South Dakotans benefit from living in the state with the lowest tax burden. It is one of just seven states with no state income tax. There is also no state *inheritance tax*, and the sales tax rate is just 4 percent, much lower than most other states.

Much of South Dakota's culture reflects the state's origins and role in the Old West. Each year, numerous fairs and events honor the state's

Native American heritage. During the summer months, arts festivals are held in Brookings and Sioux Falls. Most counties hold annual fairs, and a state fair is held in Huron, usually during late August. Sturgis is home to an annual motorcycle rally that draws more than 400,000 people.

Rural parts of South Dakota have steadily declined in population since the early 20th century. This is in part due to the decline of family farms. Some people have moved to urban areas in South Dakota, or have left the state altogether.

Major Cities

Sioux Falls is South Dakota's most populated city, with a population of about 165,000. Another 60,000 people live in the area around the city. Located in the East River region, Sioux Falls is a regional center for healthcare, business, and manufacturing, as well as for processing of agricultural products. Sioux Falls is home to cattle stockyards, slaughterhouses, and meat packaging plants. It is also

Rapid City is the second-largest in South Dakota.

has factories manufacturing plastic items and computer technology. Sioux Falls is home to the Great Plains Zoo, the Delbridge Museum of Natural History, and nearby is beautiful Palisades State Park.

Pierre is the capital of South Dakota. Pierre is located east of the Missouri River and is close to the geographic center of the state. Just over 13,000 people call Pierre home. The capital building is majestic, and its grounds include walking trails, statues, a two-acre lake, and the office of the South Dakota Historical Society. Pierre is a regional trade center as well. The Oahe Dam is located just north of Pierre.

With about 130,000 residents, *Rapid City* is the largest city of the West River region. Rapid City is close to some of South Dakota's most famous tourist attractions, including Badlands National Park, Mount Rushmore, the Crazy Horse Memorial, and Custer National Park. Tourists often stay in or near Rapid City when they are visiting these attractions.

Deadwood is a small town, with a population of just about 1,300 people, but a large reputation. This mining town was established in the 1870s during the gold rush in the Black Hills, and became known for rough and rowdy behavior. The Wild West gunman Wild Bill Hickok was shot and killed while playing poker in Deadwood in 1876. Today the city is visited by people interested in the Wild West, as well as by tourists who are interested in gambling, which is legal in Deadwood.

With a population of about 22,000, *Brookings* is South Dakota's fourth-largest city. It is home to South Dakota State University, the largest institution of higher education in the state. The city also houses the South Dakota State Art Museum and the Children's Museum of South Dakota. Each summer, an annual arts festival is held in Brookings.

Some other notable communities in South Dakota include *Aberdeen* (population 27,000), *Watertown* (pop. 22,000), and *Huron* (pop. 13,000).

Further Reading

Boyer, Crispin. *The Ultimate Road Trip*. Washington, D.C.: National Geographic Children's Books, 2012.

Perish, Patrick. *South Dakota*. Minneapolis: Bellwether Media, 2014.

Petersen, Christine. *South Dakota: Past and Present*. New York: Rosen, 2011.

Internet Resources

http://news.sd.gov/about.aspx

This site contains news about the state of South Dakota.

http://bensguide.gpo.gov/3-5/state/southdakota.html

The Ben's Guide site contains interesting and quick facts about South Dakota.

http://history.sd.gov

The website of the South Dakota State Historical Society contains interesting information about South Dakota's past and present.

 # Text-Dependent Questions

1. What was the result of the Battle of Little Bighorn?
2. What are two important issues facing South Dakota in the 21st Century?
3. Why are national parks and Mount Rushmore important to South Dakota's economy?

 # Research Project

Imagine you are a reporter sent to the site of the Battle of Wounded Knee in 1890. Read about the battle, and write a newspaper article based on what happened there. (Like a good journalist, be sure to include the five Ws: who, what, when, where, and why!) End with a paragraph explaining what you think is important for the rest of the country to understand about this battle.

Index

Numbers in **bold italics** refer to captions.

Series Glossary of Key Terms

bicameral—having two legislative chambers (for example, a senate and a house of representatives).

cede—to yield or give up land, usually through a treaty or other formal agreement.

census—an official population count.

constitution—a written document that embodies the rules of a government.

delegation—a group of persons chosen to represent others.

elevation—height above sea level.

legislature—a lawmaking body.

precipitation—rain and snow.

term limit—a legal restriction on how many consecutive terms an office holder may serve.